Colorful Cities, LLC
1329 N 47th Street #31664
Seattle WA 98103
www.colorfulcities.com | info@colorfulcities.com

100% designed, illustrated and printed in the United States of America.

ISBN: 978-0-9898972-5-9
Library of Congress Control Number: 2021910183

Concept, Design & Text: Laura Lahm
Art Direction: Jenna Ashley
Illustrations: Amelia Lea
Copy Assistance: Leigh Harrington

For more cities in the Explore & Color series please visit colorfulcities.com

A few great ways to *Explore & Color* Boston, whether you're in the city or at home!

- Create a contest to explore as many of Colorful Boston's locations as possible.

- Look for the grasshopper that tops a famous Boston building.

- Page Roulette! Turn to a random page and let the illustration be your starting point to explore or color.

- Create a scavenger hunt based on the illustrations.

- Drop your pencil on the map and explore the nearest location to your landing point or color that illustration.

- If you are in Boston, use the map and index to plan an itinerary based upon your favorite illustrations.

- See if you can visit all the locations only using the T (subway/train) or your feet!

- Color an illustration then explore its history in more depth.

- See if you can find the statue of the author who wrote the poem "The Raven" in 1845.

- Use these pages as art for your walls. Perforations at the top of the pages make this easy to do!

Are we missing one of your favorite locations in Boston? It's your turn to create the adventure! Use the designated page at the end of the book to draw your favorite place to explore in Boston and don't forget to add it to the map.

Are you ready to explore Boston?

The most important number in Boston's rich history is not 43 (the length of Boston HarborWalk's continuous, coastal pedestrian path in miles), 294 (the number of stone steps one must climb to get to the top of the Bunker Hill Monument), or 2 (how many lanterns Robert Newman hung at Old North Church to signal to Paul Revere on the eve of the American Revolution), but 1630, the year the city was founded by John Winthrop and a small group of Puritans, who had set sail from England seeking religious freedom in North America. Without this number, we would not have the rest.

This city has an incredible amount to offer for a wide variety of interests. For history buffs, Boston is home to a number of the country's firsts including: the country's first public park (Boston Common), the first grammar school (Boston Latin) and the first university (Harvard), the first public botanical garden (the Public Garden), the first subway system (MBTA or locally known as the "T"), and the first computer—you can still experience all of these. Outdoor enthusiasts can find adventure in the 34 stunning, mini escapes that await in the Boston Harbor Islands National Recreation Area. Sports are your passion? You're in the right place, as its four major professional teams have won a combined 38 championship titles. And, 23 unique neighborhoods—not including Cambridge and Brookline, which are cities in their own right—house a variety of unique, colorful communities with endless options for dining, shopping or grabbing a cappuccino.

Architectural and topographical remnants from the Colonial and Victorian eras give Boston its European feel, complete with cobblestones, bricks, and narrow, winding streets, once paths for livestock. But today, its diverse neighborhoods, formed by immigrant waves and countless college students that decided to stay, create a vibrant city that offers endless opportunities to explore.

Grab your sneakers and a convenient T (subway/train) pass, we're off to explore! Architecture buffs can span styles by starting at the domed, Art Deco-style Hatch Memorial Shell on the Charles River Esplanade, then cross the neoclassical Longfellow Bridge via the Red Line train. Stop in Cambridge to marvel at Frank Gehry's Stata Center, a Deconstructivist vision on MIT's campus. Educate yourself beyond the popular Freedom Trail by following the Black Heritage Trail or one of the Women's Heritage Trail's self-guided tours to understand some overlooked portions of Boston's history. Literature lover? Pay your respects to the expressive Edgar Allan Poe statue, wander a few blocks to Brattle Book Shop and then take the afternoon to bask in the tranquility of Boston Athenæum.

"Beantown," a nickname out-of-towners call Boston, speaks to an age-old, notable culinary offering: baked beans. You can still get the molasses-laced side dish at Union Oyster House or at a few restaurants featuring scratch-made American food; same for Indian Pudding, a Colonial molasses and cornmeal dessert. Other local eats to be had include lobster rolls and raw oysters, fresh seafood, Regina pizza (from its original North End location) and cannoli (found at Modern Pastry). For always changing, contemporary fare, the Rose Kennedy Greenway serves as a food truck hot spot.

Whether you have a day or a whole vacation to explore Boston, your options are vast. We've included a few of our favorite places to use as starting points, but there are no stopping points for this fabulous city, or for you. We hope you wonder and wander beyond the pages of this book.

Happy Exploring and Welcome to Boston!

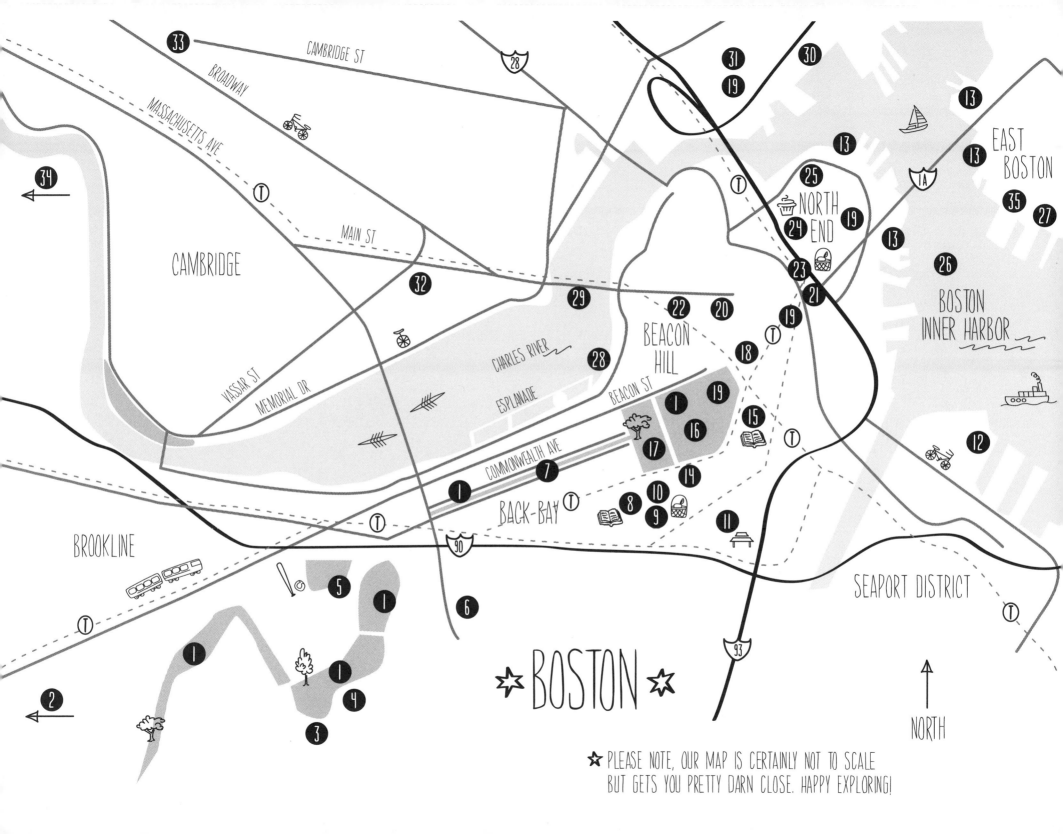

✯ BOSTON ✯

✯ PLEASE NOTE, OUR MAP IS CERTAINLY NOT TO SCALE
BUT GETS YOU PRETTY DARN CLOSE. HAPPY EXPLORING!

NORTH

CAMBRIDGE ST
BROADWAY
MASSACHUSETTS AVE
MAIN ST
CAMBRIDGE
VASSAR ST
MEMORIAL DR
CHARLES RIVER
ESPLANADE
BEACON ST
COMMONWEALTH AVE
BACK-BAY
BEACON HILL
NORTH END
EAST BOSTON
BOSTON INNER HARBOR
SEAPORT DISTRICT
BROOKLINE

COLORFUL BOSTON LOCATIONS

Please note the information was correct at the time of publication, but as with all things in life it is subject to change. Happy exploring!

ART & ARCHITECTURE

2 In Boston's Chestnut Hill community, the **Waterworks Museum**, one of the city's smallest yet most unique museums, once operated as a steam-powered pumping station from the 1890s to the 1970s, supplying residents with clean water. The old machinery is magnificent —think industrial pumps, gigantic gears and a labyrinth of pipes. The Chestnut Hill Reservoir Trail is located just across the street, so you can learn a bit of history, then get some exercise! • waterworksmuseum.org

3 Named for its mistress, patron and caretaker, the **Isabella Stewart Gardner Museum** in the Fenway neighborhood stands as a testament to one of the early 20th-century's most prolific art collectors. The museum building is modeled after a 15th-century Venetian palace, complete with an interior courtyard filled with seasonal displays of native and tropical plants. The art strongly favors the Old Masters and Gardner's collection includes pieces by Botticelli, Titian, Dürer, Rembrandt, and John Singer Sargent. gardnermuseum.org

4 The **Museum of Fine Arts**, **Boston** is one of the world's most comprehensive art museums with collections ranging from the ancient world to European Impressionists to contemporary photography. With half a million works of art in its trove, you could spend a week here and not see the same piece twice. In front of the museum's Huntington Avenue entrance, American artist Cyrus E. Dallin's bronze statue of a Native American on horseback, "Appeal to the Great Spirit," welcomes visitors. Admission includes entrance for two days, but it is also free on Wednesday evenings. • mfa.org

6 Here's a fun fact: Stand at one end of the **Mapparium** within the Mary Baker Eddy Library and whisper to your companions at the other end. Thanks to the acoustics of this spherical Back Bay treasure, they'll be able to hear you. Created out of glass by architect Chester Lindsay Churchill and then painted, the enormous, walk-through globe offers a look at the world's geographical and political climate as it was in 1935. The Eddy Library also acts as a research institute and museum centered on the life and work of Mary Baker Eddy, the author and founder of the Christian Science religion. • christianscienceplaza.com

12 Boston's Seaport neighborhood is on the rise, with new businesses, restaurants and residences appearing daily. But back in 2006, the **Institute of Contemporary Art** was one of the first to take a chance on the then-overlooked neighborhood by commissioning a brand new, 65,000 square foot home. Exhibits include innovative, visual arts from the world's leading contemporary artists. Thursday evenings are free. • icaboston.org

27 In a tucked-away corner of East Boston, **HarborArts** has integrated large-scale installations throughout 14 acres of marine industrial space. Their exhibits bring awareness to the critical role of oceans in the sustainability of the planet. Among the array of art is Karl Saliter's giant, stone-covered orb, "Apogee." • harborartsboston.com

32 For fans of Frank Gehry's postmodern, fragmented and whimsical architecture, MIT's **Ray and Maria Stata Center** in Cambridge is a must-see. The building was constructed on the former site of Building 20, a World War II-era think tank; and currently houses MIT's CSAIL (Computer Science and Artificial Intelligence Laboratory) plus the departments of philosophy and linguistics. • csail.mit.edu/about/stata-center

BOOKS, BOOKS, & MORE BOOKS

8 One of three architecturally wondrous buildings enclosing Copley Square in Back Bay, the central branch of the **Boston Public Library** presents Charles Follen McKim's turn-of-the-century vision in its Italian Renaissance Revival glory. The building itself is not the library's only work of art; in fact, it's filled with them. To start, John Singer Sargent's epic "Triumph of Religion" panels occupy a third-floor gallery. French painter Puvis de Chavannes' murals surround the main staircase, leading to Bates Hall, the library's stately reading room, with its vaulted ceiling and iconic green lamps. And don't miss the open-air central courtyard for a serene escape. Free art and architecture tours occur daily. • bpl.org

15 When independent bookstores started disappearing in the early 2000s, this nearly 200-year-old Downtown Crossing gem dug in its claws, and we are so glad it did. Filled to bursting with all styles of antiquarian and used books (more than 250,000), the **Brattle Book Shop** offers a delightful adventure through all the reads you didn't know you needed. If the weather is fair, no matter the time of year, you can browse through the discounted stacks in the adjacent parking lot. • brattlebookshop.com

18 Among travelers and residents, the **Boston Athenæum** is a delightful discovery. As one of the nation's oldest independent libraries with holdings of more than half a million volumes, it is an important asset to the city and one that's open to the public. Literature about New England history, rare books, and more make up its collections. Before you enter, be sure to take in this Beacon Hill building's gorgeous architecture. Guided tours available. bostonathenaeum.org

EATING & SHOPPING

9 From mid-May through Thanksgiving, **Copley Square Farmers Market** supplies Back Bay and South End residents with fresh produce grown at farms across the state of Massachusetts. On Tuesdays and Fridays, vendors set up stalls in picturesque Copley Square, between Trinity Church and the Boston Public Library, offering a wonderful selection of baked goods, local honey, seasonal vegetables, cut flowers, and more. massfarmersmarkets.org

11 A walk through Boston's **Chinatown** neighborhood transports you to another world, one where neighbors gather most mornings at the Chinatown Gate to play cards, sidewalk vendors sell Asian fruits and vegetables, and hanzi characters advertise where to eat all manners of Asian cuisine. This tight-knit community is the third largest Chinatown in the U.S. • boston-chinatown.info

23 The 2015 opening of **Boston Public Market** was a long time coming for city dwellers who had been asking for a year-round marketplace filled with locally and regionally sourced produce, meats, and other foodstuffs. A great place to grab lunch while exploring the Freedom Trail or shop for a handcrafted gift. • bostonpublicmarket.org

24 Closing in on a century of old-world baking in Boston's Italian-American North End enclave, **Modern Pastry** offers traditional-style Italian pastries, from lobster tails and ricotta pie to pistachio torrone and almond pizzelle. The star, however, is Modern's handmade cannoli, crispy and stuffed with sweet—but not too sweet—ricotta. Stop in for a treat and a cappuccino. • modernpastry.com

EXPLORABLE HISTORY

7 The Boston Women's Heritage Trail (BWHT) offers 13 walking tours throughout the city telling the history of great Bostonian women. One of the highlights of the Back Bay West tour, situated along the leafy Commonwealth Avenue Mall, is artist Meredith Bergmann's bronze and granite sculpture **"Boston Women's Memorial"**. It is a depiction of three influential women in Boston's history that were committed to social change: Abigail Adams, Phillis Wheatley, and Lucy Stone. • bwht.org

19 Want to take an epic journey through Revolutionary-era Boston? Follow the red-painted and/or brick line of the **Freedom Trail** from its starting point in Boston Common to 16 historical sites across Downtown, the North End and Charlestown. It takes a full day to explore its 2.5 miles and pop in at places like Old State House, Granary Burying Ground, and King's Chapel. Most sites are free. • nps.gov/bost

20 Beacon Hill's North Slope was settled by Boston's free Blacks at the turn of the 19th century. At its center, the 1806 **African Meeting House**—built entirely by free Black laborers—served as the community's church and a meeting place for local abolitionists. Today, the oldest surviving Black church building in the U.S. is a stop on the Black Heritage Trail and is the site of National Park Service historic interpretive talks. • nps.gov/boaf

21 Without a doubt one of Boston's most visited tourist attractions, **Faneuil Hall** is not to be missed, even as an off-the-beaten-path explorer. Built in 1742, it was originally given to the City of Boston as a gift from merchant Peter Faneuil. Today, this Freedom Trail site serves as the de facto headquarters for the Boston National Historical Park, and features market stalls, the Great Hall, and an artillery museum. Dozens of local and national retailers sell their wares in the surrounding marketplace, and a massive food court serves up ample lunch options. Just around the corner, Boston's historic **Custom House Tower** is now a hotel, but the spectacular views from its observation deck are still available to the public. nps.gov/bost

22 The **Lewis & Harriet Hayden House** was a critical safe house of the Underground Railroad. After escaping slavery in Kentucky, the couple moved north and settled in what is now the Beacon Hill neighborhood. Both Lewis and Harriet were anti-slavery activists, with Lewis later serving in the Massachusetts House of Representatives. More information about the Hayden House can be found on the Boston Women's Heritage Trail and the Black Heritage Trail. **Please be respectful as this is now a private residence.

30 George Washington himself named the **USS Constitution** when it first launched in 1797. She was one of the first six warships commissioned to support the newly created United States Navy, after the Revolutionary War. As the oldest warship still afloat, you can hop aboard "Old Ironsides" for free where she rests at Charlestown Navy Yard. navy.mil/local/ussconstitution

31 The Freedom Trail's last stop is also its highest point, standing 221 feet atop Breed's Hill in Charlestown. You'll notice that the **Bunker Hill Monument**'s name is actually a misnomer— the 1775 offensive by colonists against the British regulars was planned to be mounted at Bunker Hill, but colonists confused the hills and set upon the wrong summit. Ultimately, the British captured the hill, but not before losing more than 1,000 of their men. Today, visitors can ascend 294 steps to the top of the tower, but you must be hale and hearty to do so, as there's no elevator. The views, however, are worth the effort. • nps.gov/bost

33 Thousands of specimens of mammals from across the globe; David Rockefeller's grand and colorful beetle collection; 375-million-year-old fossils: these are just a few of the fascinating and dramatic exhibits mounted at **Harvard Museum of Natural History** in Cambridge. Perhaps the most unique offering is the "Ware Collection of Blaschka Glass Models of Plants", intricate and exact scientific replicas of 780 types of flowers and plants, made more than 100 years ago by hand. • hmnh.harvard.edu

PARKS & OUTSIDE ADVENTURES

1 The **Emerald Necklace** is a series of parks and green spaces stretching seven miles from Franklin Park to Boston Common. Offering more than 1,000 acres of greenery, small bodies of water and fresh air, it's the perfect place for a long run, bike or picnic with friends. • emeraldnecklace.org

13 Looking for a quiet break while still in the city? The **Boston Harborwalk** follows the crooks and crags of the coastline for nearly 43 miles, through many neighborhoods including East Boston, South Boston, the Financial District, the Waterfront, the Seaport, and Dorchester. The walkway's experiences are as diverse as the neighborhoods—find a waterside restaurant, enjoy a midday jog, or catch the sunrise over the water. bostonharborwalk.org

14 Late in 2014, accomplished sculptor Stefanie Rocknak unveiled "Poe Returning to Boston," her bronze, windblown, raven-toting depiction of the prolific poet and early writer of American horror stories. Although Poe is more closely associated with cities like Richmond, Baltimore, and New York, he was born and lived in Boston until the age of three, in a small apartment in the Theater District above what is now known as **Edgar Allan Poe Square**.

16 The neighborhoods of Beacon Hill, Back Bay, Downtown, and the Theater District meet at the centrally located **Boston Common**, the oldest public park, founded in 1634. The park serves as a gathering place on any day of the year. In winter, the Frog Pond opens for skating, and in summer, kids splash in its shallow waters. Fountains, food trucks, Frisbee, even an old cemetery, are all part of the fun. • boston.gov/parks

17 Not to be confused with Boston Common (see above) or Boston Garden (where the Celtics and Bruins used to play), the **Public Garden**, with its lush, seasonal blooms, fairytale-esque Swan Boats, and real-life swan couple, is a fitting botanical green space for the posh Back Bay neighborhood in which it resides. Established in 1837, it emanates a Victorian vibe, complete with unusual plants and whimsical fountains. Presiding over it all: an equestrian statue of George Washington—although the uninformed often think it's Paul Revere. boston.gov/parks

26 **Boston Harbor** is quintessentially associated with its infamous Tea Party revolt in 1773. Even though it's still a very active shipping port, the Harborwalk path along the shore is one of the best ways to view this area. Be sure to explore the more than 30 islands in the harbor with many being easily accessible via ferry. • bostonharborislands.org

28 Follow the Arthur Fiedler Footbridge to the **Hatch Memorial Shell** if you're heading there from Back Bay or Beacon Hill. The iconic, Art Deco concert venue is perhaps best known as the site of the Boston Pops' annual, fireworks-laden Fourth of July celebration, but other local musical organizations and radio stations host free concerts from spring through fall. There's also free, family-friendly film screenings on Friday nights in the summer. hatchshell.com

(29) **Longfellow Bridge** crosses from Boston's West End neighborhood into Cambridge and has been connecting the sister cities over the Charles River since 1901. (A previous timber bridge was built in 1793.) You may hear locals refer to the Longfellow as the "Salt and Pepper" bridge, for its four granite towers that resemble salt and pepper shakers. While riding the T Red Line is the most common way to cross; walking, biking and driving are options too. Enjoy the spectacular views!

(35) There are many places throughout the city to get incredible Boston views of the harbor, the Charles River and old architecture alongside modern structures. A few of our favorite locations that offer different perspectives: the top of the Bunker Hill Memorial, the shores of Pier's Park and from the 14th floor of the Observation Deck at Independence Wharf.

SPORTS & EVENTS

(5) The oldest ballpark in Major League Baseball™, **Fenway Park**™ was built in 1912 and has been home to the Boston Red Sox™—and their diehard fans—ever since. Attend a game and pay your respects to the famed Green Monster™ (the left-field wall that has thwarted many a home run), the manually operated scoreboard, and the displays of artifacts from former players. You don't have to miss out if it isn't baseball season—Fenway™ offers guided tours year-round. • mlb.com/redsox

(10) The **Boston Marathon** is the world's oldest annual marathon and one of the most prestigious global running events. The course runs through neighboring communities and ends at Copley Square in the heart of Boston. Be sure to check out Nancy Schön's, "Tortoise and Hare" sculpture on the Square as a tribute to the many runners worldwide that participated over the years. • baa.org

(25) Every summer, the North End comes alive with vibrant weekly festivals and processions held in honor of Roman Catholic saints. The neighborhood's Italian residents parade down streets with statues, floats, and blessed relics, and then celebrate with a feast or a festival. Started in 1919, **St. Anthony's Feast** is the region's largest Italian religious festival and takes place over four days at the end of August. Vendors sell traditional foods, from arancini to zeppole, and musicians play live. It's free to attend. • stanthonysfeast.com

(34) During the penultimate weekend in October, thousands of spectators line both the Boston and Cambridge banks of the Charles River to cheer on rowers and teams as they race the three-mile course of the world-renowned **Head Of The Charles® Regatta**. Bring a picnic, join an alfresco Harvard student cocktail party, or visit the official rowing and fitness expo near the finish line. • hocr.org

NOTES:

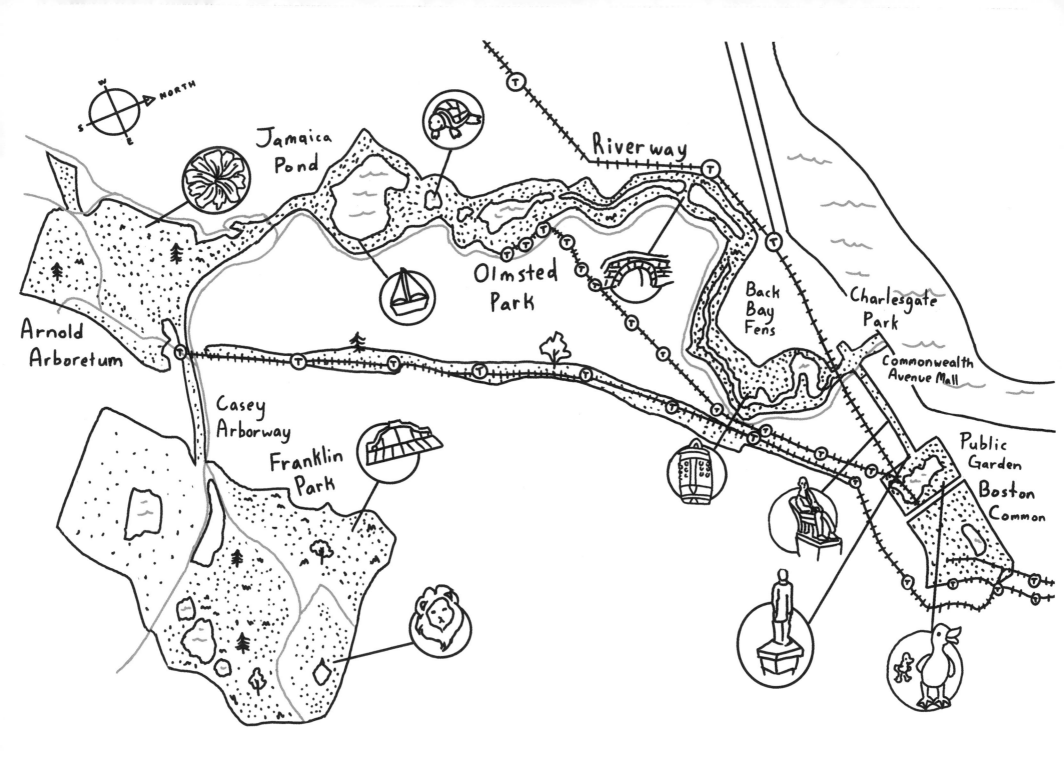

EMERALD NECKLACE

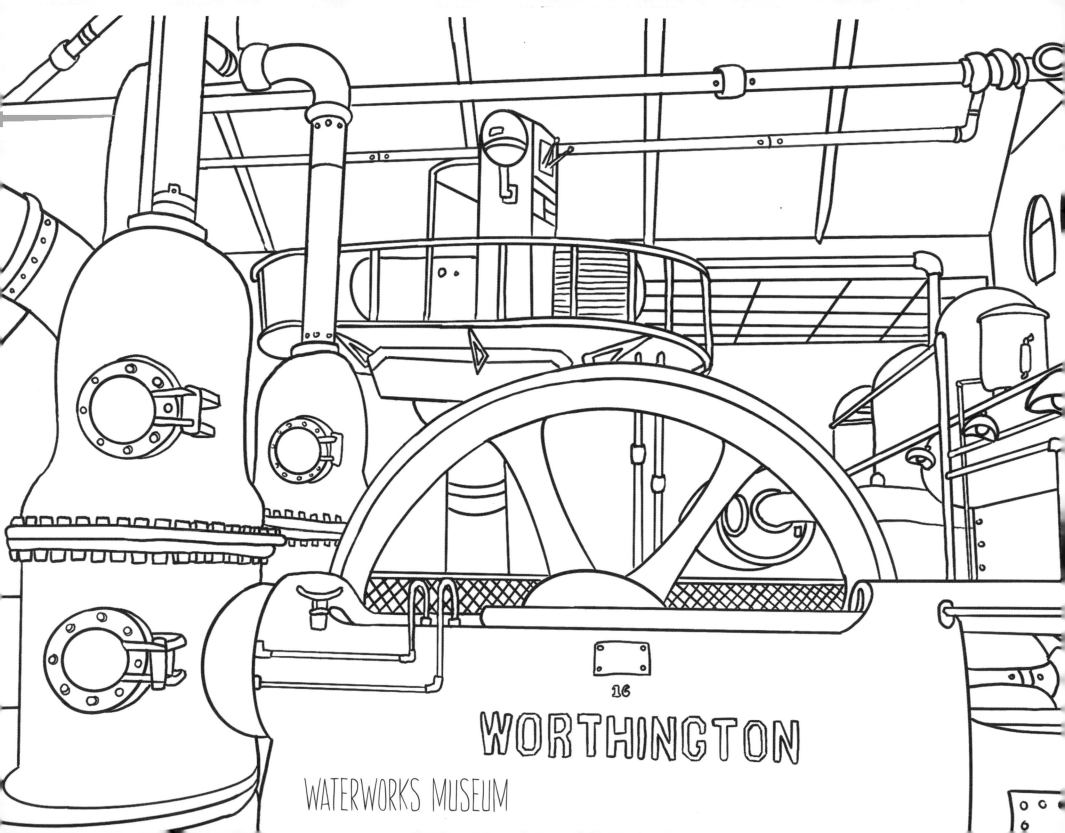

WORTHINGTON

16

WATERWORKS MUSEUM

ISABELLA STEWART GARDNER MUSEUM

MVSEVM OF FINE ARTS

Courtesy of Museum of Fine Arts, Boston

FENWAY PARK

ANTIC

MAPPARIUM

BOSTON PUBLIC LIBRARY

Fresh Jam $7 ea.

HOME GROWN KALE $4/lb

POTATOES $2/lb

LOCAL HONEY

4 $/lb

BOK CHOY $3/lb

strawberries

$4/lb

MUSHROOMS

COPLEY SQUARE FARMERS MARKET

CHINATOWN

INSTITUTE OF CONTEMPORARY ART

HARBORWALK

EDGAR ALLAN POE SQUARE

BOSTON COMMON

PUBLIC GARDEN

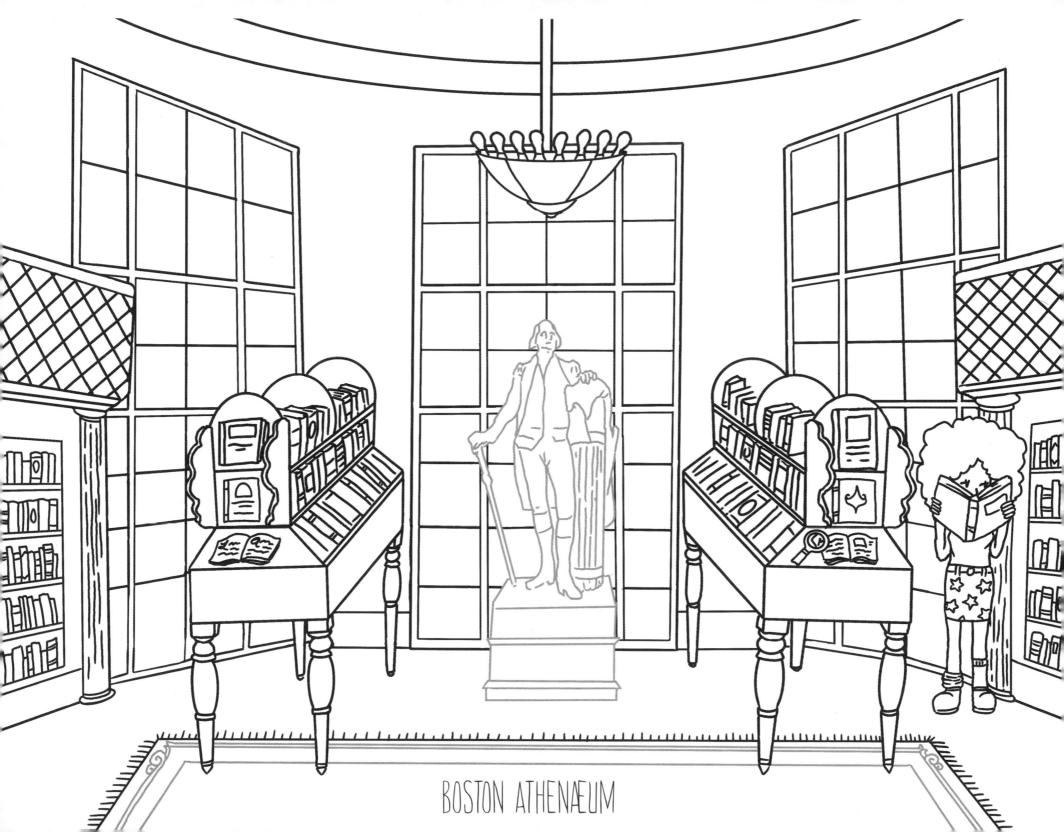

BOSTON ATHENÆUM

AFRICAN MEETING HOUSE

FANEUIL HALL & CUSTOM HOUSE TOWER

LEWIS & HARRIET HAYDEN HOUSE

BOSTON PUBLIC MARKET

MODERN PASTRY

ST. ANTHONY'S FEAST

BOSTON HARBOR

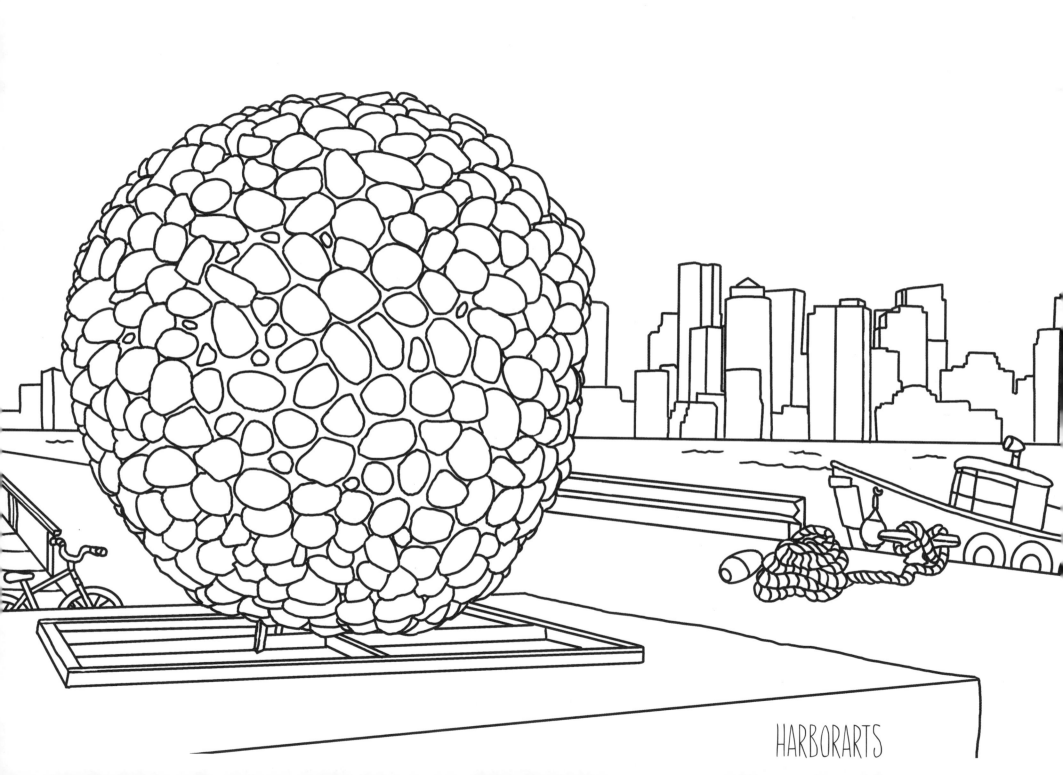

HARBORARTS

HATCH SHELL

LONGFELLOW BRIDGE

MONUMENT

BUNKER HILL MONUMENT

MIT—STATA CENTER

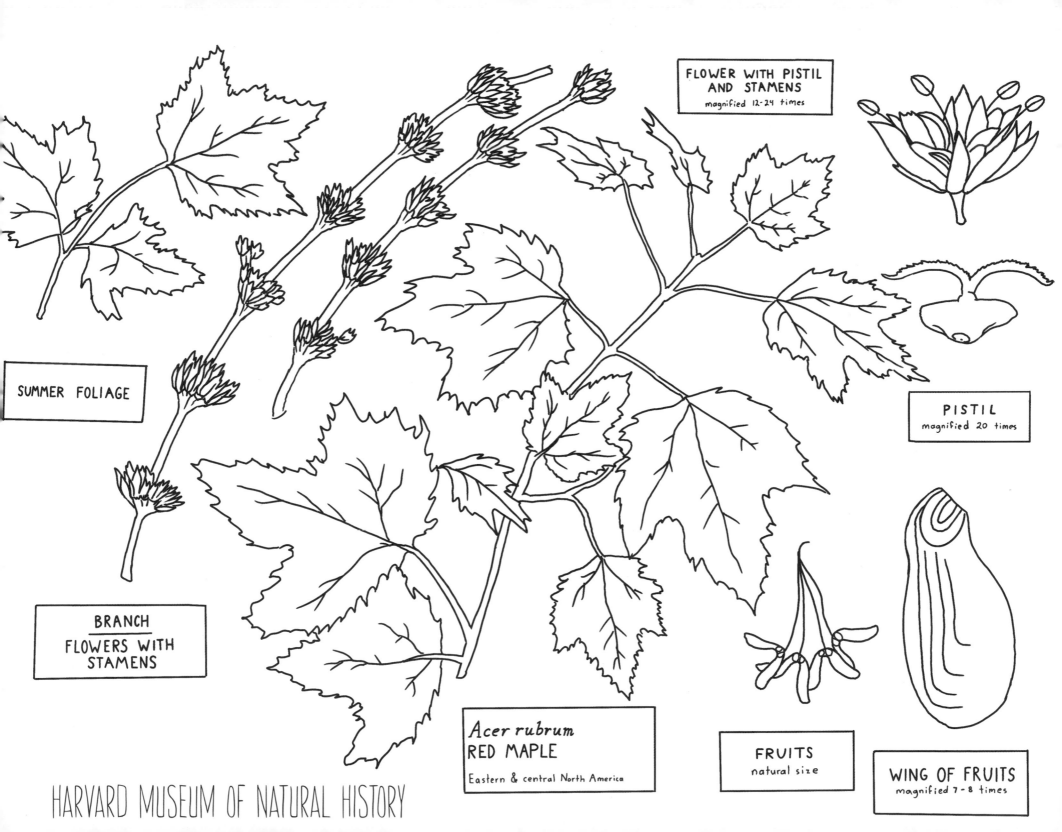

FLOWER WITH PISTIL
AND STAMENS
magnified 12-24 times

SUMMER FOLIAGE

PISTIL
magnified 20 times

BRANCH
FLOWERS WITH
STAMENS

Acer rubrum
RED MAPLE

Eastern & central North America

FRUITS
natural size

WING OF FRUITS
magnified 7 - 8 times

HARVARD MUSEUM OF NATURAL HISTORY

HEAD OF THE CHARLES REGATTA

BOSTON

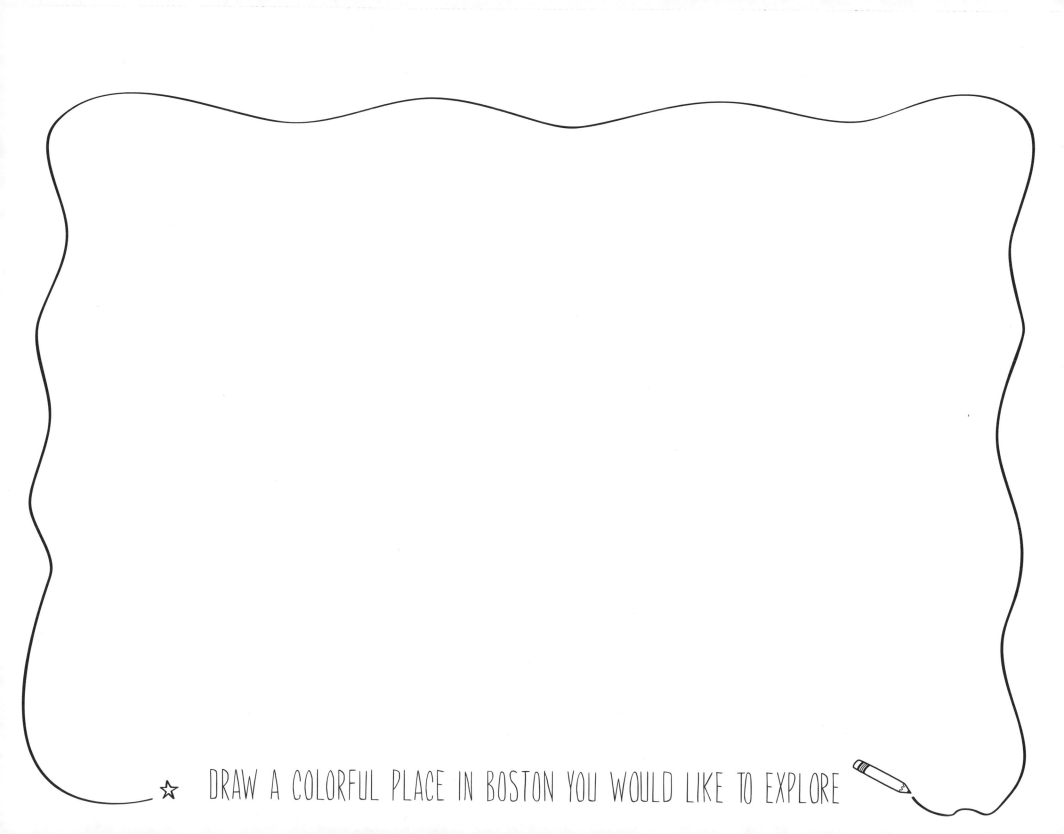

DRAW A COLORFUL PLACE IN BOSTON YOU WOULD LIKE TO EXPLORE